IN THE OCTOPUS NURSERY

IN THE OCTOPUS NURSERY

Geoff Bowman

PT Poetry Press

Box 1514

Port Townsend WA 98368

Acknowledgments

This volume was assisted down the birth canal and printed by the University Book Store publishing program.

Some of the poems have been published or accepted by *Is* and *Minotaur.*

There are two people without either of whom you, dear reader, would be holding a bundle of blank sheets of paper, and I a daydream. One is Jane Evans, whose love and inspiration tore the veil and showed me truth. The other is Lee Faulkner, cyber-warrior and enthusiast, who would not let me go halfway.

There are other names I would call out in gratitude—if you don't know what you did, I surely do: Bruce Bode, Phil Montenegro, Bryn Bowman, Ruth Apter, Bill Mawhinney, and Louise who tends the graves. Thank you all.

CONTENTS

Snowflakes

Finalities

MUSE

i hand you the page
of newly taken words
and silence rises
turning us to islands

you watch the words move
i watch your
eyebrows leap, eyes blink
half-smile flicker candle-like
even (o muse) a tear

you are not always
my best critic, your love
is too gentle but you are
my first, wanting the baby
tenderly welcomed to life

later submission, rejection, typos
the whole churning poetry industry
for now i try to read
my words on your face
my heart in yours

Cuttings

OPEN MIC

a poem strapped to each leg
he kicks open the swinging doors
and backlit by the sun strides
into the coffeehouse

the other poets look up
aware of the disturbed air
judging the size of his mind
by the size of his hat

sizing him up, sensing he knows
about birdsong, his father's death
and the cool stillness
of the shed's darkness

one by one they sidle
behind the rail fence
the bartender swings open the gate
and lets in the bull

slobber dangling from his red mouth
one horn-tip broken off
dried blood darkening
the ancient break

wait! shouts one poet *no bull!*
let's see him handle this . . .
a thrown pencil skitters
across the grimy floor

he bends, picks it up, notices
the yellow paint, the number two
the eraser all but used up

and begins to read

THE POINTE, A GATED COMMUNITY

one of the things we really liked
about the pointe was the security entrance
and its 24-hour attendant staff

we overlooked the extra "e"
to have the peace of mind that comes
from defining and excluding the riff-raff

but one day about a month ago
as i tried to drive past the gatehouse
i noticed antonio was not on duty

though it was his usual day
and i saw two men, both armed
had replaced him—the bearded one

with cold eyes told me no one
was allowed to leave and when i asked why
he told me i and the other residents

had so much money that we endangered
the welfare of society as a whole
i mean have you ever heard of such a thing

i worked hard investing my family's money
and this fidel castro lookalike tells me
deborah and i are a threat to his homeless friends

i made the tires squeal in a u-turn
and headed straight home for my pistol
but couldn't find it, talked to next-door-jim

who couldn't find his either—was it the maids? the yardmen?
the guy who chlorinated the pool but couldn't habla ingles?
we never found out. before the cable stopped

the news implied we weren't the only community
locked behind a 24-hour entrance now staffed
with semi-automatics and called a checkpoint

the dogs are gone, even the small ones
and the frozen vegetables. the dogfood too
though no one admits it. the cats left as a group

almost right away. just one morning there weren't any.
we don't socialize much—really we avoid each other.
we thought it would be temporary

just pay a few more taxes. i'm not so sure now.
jim didn't make it. they hunted him.
i don't feel secure any more.

ONLY NEVADA

they came from a town called only, nevada
named after the store
where two highways meet
at a rusty stopsign—
it's the only store in 65 miles
of snow-streaked violet mountain ranges
and advertises *cafe, lodging, gas* and *slots*
it doesn't mention assorted taxidermy
and a sportsman's club of AK-47 owners

she was one and brought the rest
coffee and cleavage and brassy gold hair
she loved peanut brittle and him
the two of them would be enough
for most towns—in the echoing emptiness of only
they pushed the wide open spaces
farther apart.   she claimed to have grown up
on a dairy farm but had learned somewhere
how to milk the bull. he was a riverboat gambler
in a laptop age. they thought out loud.
he once asked a one-man traveling rodeo
who stopped for gas if he knew the difference
between farmer boots and cowboy boots
volunteering after a period of silence
farmer boots the shit's on the outside

cleaning up the breakage that
could be cleaned up took her a good two hours
but we saw her suppress a smile
with the first words of his question

one time they went away *for valentine's day* he said
and returned a week or three later
with a sign in the pickup bed that read
our on-site crematorium
means you'll never have to wonder
who's handling your loved one

it had the name of a funeral farm in wickenburg
he said the sign just looks better out here
away from big-city crowding
but most folks call it creepy

if you come to only
you might check for a big red pickup
out behind the store
when it's there you can always
just keep driving

WELCOME TO OUR BEACHES

i don't know how anyone can live right next to the ocean
the constant whispering of the waves would drive me nuts
and i don't suppose waves wonder if their lives have a purpose
though they certainly could—i mean look at it, they arise
somewhere incredibly far away
japan maybe, and cross the whole ocean
to hit the shore here, pssssshhh, in between two other waves
each of which goes pssssshhh and is done
how can you take pride in your work if that's all you do
i think it's likely waves are actually profoundly depressed
and "oh shit" "goddamn it" and "is that all" are good translations
of that shushing sound they make on the gravel beach
above which i sit waiting for it to be noon,
and wondering just what is the big deal about
waterfront property anyway

A POEM WITH BIRDS IN IT

a slipperysteep roof
   a towering flue
      that has no screen or bend
         then birds descend

(intending what
   i can't imagine) to end up
      in the woodstove firebox
         unable to fly up

as far as they had rattled down—
   coming to a chilly home
      i pick up some kindling
         open the iron gates

and find three
   sitting in ashes
      on the grate, sleepy-eyed
         dozing away the darkness

—finches, i think—
   before each by each darts by my head
      toward the cabin-enclosed light behind me—
         we yank the door wide open

as if warmth
   were what we'd be rid of
      not birds
         frantically thumping their reflections

scattering their ashes—
   the first finds an exit rather quickly
      later, exhausted with chasing
         the other two

i beat one to death
　　with a kindling stick
　　　　and toss the loose feathery body
　　　　　　outside—the third

we can't find
　　until morning streaming in
　　　　as ever wakes us
　　　　　　to terror fluttering in a yellow eye

OFF THE LEASH

near a sleeping body
they say the spirit wanders not far,
like a leashed dog
and they may be right
because this morning i found
the unexpected.   the first i knew
was when i swung my feet off the bed
to the floor and felt the answering sway
of breasts on my chest.   then i couldn't feel
my balls on the sheet, there was nothing
there, well not nothing, but a soft place
and the perfume of satisfaction.   forget getting up
to pee—how did this happen?   i turned to you
and there you were, looking quite puzzled
at being in a body familiar to me
if not to you and i knew
a mirror would say to you too: how did
this happen?   i recalled our night.   strangely
i remembered being penetrated, how i stretched my legs apart
and pivoted my hips up to meet your downward thrust
and draw you deeper into me, and i feel right now
the residual soreness from all the friction it took
to separate you from your last drops.
it isn't enough to stop me
wanting you, wanting us now.
so with no other solution in sight
i walked to my body in your body
slipped it over whoever's cock that is
and began the gentle movements
that would bring us where
things got confused last night.
hope this works

SIGHTSEEING

oh sir
you remember me?
i saw you yesterday in mumbai
you have such money
i ask you gi' me
only one dollah
yesterday you say tomorrow
sir you remember me?

you remember?
i saw you yesterday in lagos
i ask you medicine
little medicine
yesterday you do hurry
yesterday you say tomorrow
sir you remember me?

remember me?
i saw you yesterday in juarez
let me follah you
please sir
i want home and work
i keep eyes down
yesterday you say tomorrow
sir you remember me?

COLONIALISM: A BRIEF HISTORY

the pale man
races his land rover along
the jungle road
rounds a blind corner
too fast to see
a native walking
bouncing
off the windshield and over

skids to a stop   *my god*
runs back with his notepad
and issues a ticket for
failure to yield to
oncoming traffic
sticks it between
the toes of a twisted foot

BILL OF RIGHTS

you have the right to change your mind
if you can still find it
after the excesses of your midlife crisis

you have the right to burrow into me
like an IV i forgot in my arm for twenty years
until you yanked it out to remind me

you have the right to use our connection
to nourish yourself alone
to suck and drain and weaken me

you have the right to leave abruptly
and to smash everything you can reach
along your pathway to the door

you have the right to get out, and keep on getting out
even as my breasts erupt in tumors
and i need you more than ever

you have the right to look after your needs
first and forever, to take as much time
and as many women as necessary

you have the right not to mean a damn word you say
and to sleep with an untroubled conscience
while i thrash, pound the pillow and shout your name

you have the right to be found
in the brush that lines the side of the highway
facedown while the animals cautiously approach

whatever we said, some other time, it
just doesn't count now that you have the right
to look at me across a room as though

you almost remember who i am

SHERIFF'S LOG

Note: The factual context for this series of poems, as well as some of the italicized words and phrases, depends upon the Jefferson County Sheriff's Log as reported in the weekly town newspaper.

1) THE METHOD

this has always been a lonely neighborhood
even more now that jake passed, a knock
at the door is a rare event.
over a year ago there was a rapping
but when i opened the door there was no one.
after a while it happened again.   then again.
it wasn't till i kept track of dates
that i realized they had a method
and always came at dusk on the third
tuesday of the month, don't ask me why

the next month i hid in the yard but no one came
until an hour after i went to bed and then
the knocking and the sound of running feet.
well, i wouldn't call them *suspects*
they're just people—and no, i'm not scared
i find after jake died i'm not frightened of anything
any more, i just called to report my concerns
and to ask you if anybody, anybody else
was having similar trouble

2) CLINT

this old man in a big pickup
rear-ended the lady stopped
in front of him, never touched
his brakes and while she
called the police decided
to make his getaway
with his radiator *blowing steam*
pursued by a deputy
who estimated their speed at
twelve miles an hour then
went around him, blocked him off

sitting in the unmoving vehicle
the man raced away in the film he saw
where he and clint eastwood traded lives

his wife sat silent in the shotgun seat
thinking how he'd always been like this
and if she just looked out the window
she wouldn't be there

3) THE DEPUTY SPEAKS

my wife grew up in appalachia so nothing i bring home
from the job surprises her, even the woman who called to report
wild rabbits on the loose. i spent my youth in westwood.
there it was serve and protect. here? i gotta tell you it feels like
humor and protect. see, a guy goes for a walk
and when he comes home the door to his house is open.
somehow (he said it was *years of experience*)
he knows homeland security left it that way, so he calls us.

it's like a home way out here comes with a membership
in a citizen's army against strange events. suppose
unknown people attach electronic controlling devices
to your car. you just drive it to the sheriff's office
and if, after mike nearly ruins his shirt
scooting under it, he says that's the ground
wire for a stereo amp, you thank him politely
and leave. if *two unknown men are tying a cable*
to my bed while i'm in it, the phone's right there and so are we.
sometimes we're stretched between the *woman bitten*
by her own cat while feeding it and the
items falling from the sky on state route 116.

and the *stop sign removed and replaced with one in arabic?*
i drove out and saw that one myself.
there it was. i think that's arabic.

4)   INCIDENT REPORT

A Port Hadlock man reportedly assaulted himself on April 16.

they stood beside the prowl car and watched the guy
with the jerky movements of a furious puppet
pound with his clenched fists
his thighs, his shoulders, his soft belly
his face already marked by blood
trickling from his nose, his breath
gasping

the deputies looked at one another
this kind of call the first thing you do
is break up the fight

just beyond the cone of light from the streetlamp
there seemed to be people standing
who cast no shadows

"bastard—did you think you could
treat me like that (thud)
forever and i'd do
(whack) nothing?"

5) PETS

he walked in with it under his arm
hanging to the floor either side of his wrist

you always tell me she continued *i have a dog*
because i can't sustain a relationship with you—
what the hell is that?   it's moving!

it's a python.   i found it at teal lake.
i was fishing.   i want to keep it.

just what does that say about what
you can't sustain?   what does it eat anyway?

i don't know he said *i'll call 911, they'll tell me*

6) THE POWER OF WORDS

she was in the safeway and didn't even know
what she did but a man called her
stupid so she left her cart
right in the aisle, walked out front
to the phone and called the sheriff

you're in trouble now buster
you can't talk to people like that

while across town *his step-daughter swore at him*
called him a fucking asshole if you must know
while i give her a roof to live under
is that legal?

and in the middle of answering that question
a woman told 911 a man said *hello*
to her, oh and also *it's a nice evening*
she didn't know why
it just seemed suspicious

the deputy was explaining to the dispatcher
how the moon affects people's behavior
when last night's woman in port ludlow
who had reported *a strange vibration*
under her bed during the night called to ask
when the investigating officer would arrive

the deputy looked at the dispatcher
i guess i'll take that one he said

7) THE CHASTITY POLICE

i can't help it if i was raised right.
nowadays children aren't brought up
so much as corralled, so if i see
plastic forks stuck handle-first
into my lawn or a box of dirt
that wasn't there yesterday in the yard
or *a couple embracing beside the road*
you can bet i'm calling it in

oh i've heard the old saw that pentecostals
never have sex standing up because
it can lead to dancing but when my binoculars
confirmed the girl next door was running nude
in her house i demanded the sheriff
come out himself to restore
some semblance of the order
that disappeared just before
i became a young woman

Coupling

TO LOVE

gimme a lot of that little by little
a little bit more of that much too much

releasing a slow rainy saturday
reading erotic poems aloud by turns

every so often lay the book down
and sit on the edge of this

continent, take a few
hesitant fingersteps, lipsteps

every so often pick up the book
in soft paper cover feeling so much

like skin and read again
lines lasting all afternoon o love do

gimme a lot of that little by little
a little bit more of that much too much

JUST DIFFERENT, THAT'S ALL

they say when a new and important romance begins
a man gets a gym membership
a woman tells her girlfriends
first, and then her mother

they say when love enters the scene
a man acts like nothing has changed
a woman knows everything has

they say when a new couple forms
a man wants everyone to know she's his
a woman wants another week or year
of privacy to see if this love is true

they say meeting the parents is a watershed event
what about grown children, the buddies, the salon staff
all the ones to whom you'll have to explain
why it didn't work or why it did?

they say a man makes no big announcements but
assumes everyone will notice, while a woman
sees her face and his on billboards,
on coins in her purse and the evening news

ONE MORE

she selects the perfect pair of panties
to lie in a moist and crumpled heap
on the floor

bending forward
brassiere cups
are like hands, supporting
so she replaces it with a gray silk camisole

the feel of the fabric is
being touched everywhere

sure he is not sitting with a beer
watching the afternoon game
before showering and changing shirts

she feels the button and the hole lock together
in her blouse, anticipates her hands almost fumbling
making them come undone

he imagines he has time
for one more

CORSAGE

i fancy up faster than when i was young—
it's a series of habits, you know, the makeup,
and i don't loiter in front of mirrors now that

only so much can be done to unwind time—
so though he isn't due for another ten minutes
i'm already poised in the reading chair

i'd rather sit on the edge of the furniture
like a jumper on the ledge
thinking it over—fifty years

and we still use the same words: *date*
and *boyfriend* for now, for now.   he can't
hold a candle to robert but i don't want

to be just a widow forever.   and so i am an actor
in this farce, this shadow dance
of highschool recalled, though it's different—

if the boy was late then, i didn't worry his brain had exploded
in a stroke, or that the great weight on his chest
crushed his heart, or that he just forgot where i live

and if we "get physical" (as the young call
the inconceivable) i may even know the last time is
the last, and find it easier to let go.

so it might be good to see him.   we can talk
about other things.   and sometimes he looks at me
with a glow in his eyes even robert didn't have.

FOR FLOYD, AGE 82, AND LEONA, AGE 97, ENGAGED IN JEFFERSON COUNTY

you and i, we met in an emergency room
i was the blind man juggling
you were the gymnast with a broken leg
who hadn't been here before
we laughed to find one another
i had my ways of seeing, you had yours
what were we doing here anyway
they couldn't heal us separately
nor comprehend our union

strangers watch us promenade
hand in hand, a medallion of happiness
do any suspect we just now met
after dreaming of meeting all
our lives and never meeting
though sustaining a crazy willingness
to jump out the boat and run cross water
if it seemed the distant beach might be
the one sought so long and faithfully

hearing the sounds from behind
blown curtains of our beach cabin
young folks are sometimes frightened
sometimes curious about the tingle
of northern delights sweeping over
and over our mingled bodies, how
like kids after rain we can stomp
in every ingathered puddle in
the whole damn parking lot

too late they say how could it be
too late to fall in love when each touch
unravels the love knot and every breath
struggles to live enough that when
we reach that narrow valley
you'll be with me—declaring
it's too late not to fall in love

THE COMPLIANT LOVER'S COMPLAINT

you asked me to
not just once
many times
to love you like this

i didn't know
you were calling me
you never used my name
called me someone

i want someone to
i wish someone would
i never knew
it was me

you never said
touch me like that
kiss me there
nice girls don't say that

they wait alone
for someone
no one knows he is—
you could have told me

told me *love me*
with all you've got
and wakened the neighbors
calling my name

MADONNA

i can't remember which one of you
i was nursing in the photo
i pretend i do but really
i have no idea at all

you may have been my first
which would account for the faint hysteria
around my eyes and the fear
i would be sucked dry down
to a windblown husk of myself

or could have been later in the nearly endless
alternation of fucking and feeding
which would explain the bored glance
so easily taken for meditative calm

it doesn't matter to me and didn't then
though each of you and your father had
your own obsessive enthrallment by
the twinned abundance of a woman's body

and squandered so awfully much effort
to peer discreetly down blouses and up cap sleeves
and study the pictures in the scrap lumber clubhouses
where real girls weren't allowed

later i knew how you strained
almost wrestled your date
to get past a kiss to a handful
and how you studied unfastening
a brassiere   using only   one hand
and i remembered his grasping lips
nuzzled into my chest

i wanted, and wanted him to be
as intensely interested in my heart
as in them, at least to recognize i was
here and able to hold and nourish

your own in a darkened bedroom
while you tiptoed home late from
wherever pointed breasts had led you
and slipped into our bed
asking the holy mother
for soft forgiveness

THE LOVER UNDERESTIMATES HIS BELOVED

of all things small
you are the least consequential
an array of crystalline atoms
making a sparkle of light
almost too tiny to notice

you are the shake of spice
that flavors the whole
the slightest deviation in course
that drags the interstellar probe
lightyears away from its goal

when i am not near you
you are the gleam in my eye
that everyone almost notices
sensing that something is different
unable to quite say why

in six and a half billion
you are but one
and that overlooks all the unborn
who are not like you
and will not be when all is done

you are a single breath of fresh air,
a passing thought, a short
memory for pain now forgot,
in the compass a tiny tingle
in setting that finds safe port

you are the butterfly's wing
concocting tornadoes,
a bright spark in the phoenix's ash,
the only value that stays
when all the markets crash

you are the single drop of ink
staining all the water, the faint ring
that might be angels singing
and though you are everywhere i
look i can hardly find you

MARILYN

we are in the marilyn monroe room
in the el trovatore motel in kingman arizona
and i am watching you sleep

every wall has at least one picture of
marilyn. you drowse under the classic
blown-up skirt shot that reveals

a sedate pair of white cotton underwear, so virginal
so something your maiden aunt might wear—
but surely not with marilyn's expression

head tilted back, eyes closed, and lips
between a smile and a gasp as she feels
hot subway breath on her stocky legs

now i remember why JFK lay awake
in the lincoln bedroom, thinking of her
and touching himself, why young warriors

in europe and korea carried her photo
not one of their actual girlfriends
until she dissolved like the tablets

in her blood and the erotic flame flared in a million sparks
one like you resting after love, your breath burning
this route 66 motel to the ground

MOSES' BASKET

when pharaoh's daughter heard a baby
wailing over the water
she sent her attendants
wading in muck and rushes
until they found him
and brought him out
in a basket

no one talks about the basket or
what became of it
was it forgotten
on the muddy bank
or did one of the girls
take it home
to hold kindling
for the fire
or vegetables on market day?

that was what it was made for
as i am made to hold
you in my arms
floating
into this morning

HOODOO

i found your shirt
your little spaghetti-strap top
way in the back
of the dryer and i thought

if i turn this inside out
and hang it at the head
of your side of the bed
maybe you'll return

when i walked around the bed
to put tacks in the wall
for your shirt i found that
single sock you missed
last week and i thought

if i get my
solo sock
and lay yours across it
so as to make a cross
maybe you'll return

later in the sink
i saw a couple of your hairs
and a trimmed fingernail
and i thought

of that old juju woman who lived
by the tracks just around
that corner no one went round and
knew what i wanted
was a power to bring you back
whenever i wanted

not you yourself, surely not your clothes
scattered all over my apartment
but the abolition of helplessness

and turned on the water
and washed the hairs away

44

Snowflakes

THE BLOCKHOUSE

the blockhouse
in which
the pain is kept
as if
it were precious
has a gate
so
low and so
narrow
only a child
can crawl in
and say
it's safe
to come out
and live

THE FOURTH

i hate fireworks she said *they remind me*
of gunshots her age, race and class saying everything
about whether she'd heard a gun fired in anger

i ignored her for moonrise,
awaiting the start of the show:
a hundred long-petalled chrysanthemums

bloomed in the blasted night.
i saw a weeping willow made entirely
of glowing orange sparks. explosions scattered

white-hot balls that winked out one by one
like the stars on judgment day. the sky sizzled
and smoked, burning fragments drifted east

on the wind. i thought she'd stay silent.
they should cancel the fourth of july, it really stresses
the animals. there's liberalism in a nutshell

no birthday party for america because of pets. do you know
in spite of all the talk about their loyalty not one dog
signed the declaration of independence?

and when it was time to draft a constitution
the cats were asleep atop all the important papers? no
we as a nation don't owe them anything. let them cower

under the bed one night a year. afterwards the streets
are so empty it seems everyone might be
under the bed. that's alright. tonight i say

unashamedly *boom, pow* without hesitation, totally
blam and still have room on my tongue to
praise beauty in the technicolor sky

SEVEN DAYS

in the beginning it was dark and kind of lonely
you think i don't get lonely but i do, and dark?
as dark as the innards of complete nonexistence

couldn't see anything, not heaven, not earth
if i hadn't made the surface of the deep be wet
my spirit wouldn't know what it hovered over

it got to be bothersome so i created light
and could see to arrange things—day and night,
sky and dry land, it took most of three days

but turned out pretty good, i never had to
change much. a flood, eclipses, i know
and i added some decorative stuff, like stars,

birds, plants with seeds, fish, people, all
good ideas but the farther i went the less i liked it
always preferring the time when there was only

the whisper of mountain erosion, the scraping
of continents against each other, the endless
slap of empty waves so restful after all

TRINITY

One

The one in charge.
Father who knows best.
When He rides in
the town watches behind drawn blinds
Him walk through a doorway
leaving no space for anyone else.
Placate Him. If He wants to He
will bring pain, endless butchery if He wants,
no explanation offered, not even a Name.
It is His seed always takes root
His garden, His creation,

His omnipotence, accepting only
obedience and worship.
Some say He is the ego deified
and we'd all be gods if we could. He breeds
the recovering Catholic, the jack Mormon,
the materialist, doesn't give a damn if you abandon
His altars, knows there are no others, knows why
logic and science and communism
became religions. *I'm not askin' you,
I'm tellin' you.* Mean without even drinking,
a hard hand pounds the child's buttocks,
quick to molest and torture, leaving
only the hope that all we see
is what we think about what we see.

two

carried in his mother's arms, he melts
into the crowd and an unwritten
history but no one forgets the eyes
of the firstborn of a pair of wetbacks

years passed with the same old mercilessness
we hoped for love and were lucky to get justice
until he showed up looking just like anyone
except willing to take the bullet without thinking,
passing out a bag of gifts, interceding, saving
sheltering even against the father's fury
always busy with the work of love. maybe he gave
some lust-driven preacher a golden mercedes, but heck
he's just a boy with a boy's weakness for cool cars.

when it counted, when we needed someone
on our bond, he was always there
and here too. maybe we didn't deserve it, maybe we didn't
have to. maybe that's how strong love is and crucifixion
was our accident, he even said so
and asked that all be forgiven.

as he grew toward that, the stories collected (he was the boy
quarterback who threw a fish five hundred yards)
and became harder to keep straight, more outrageous,
got the attention of the usually drunk and drowsy
authorities who almost hung up the wrong man

in the end it was the words that buried him alive.   there's a village
in japan where the peasants will take you
to his grave and, for a slight additional fee
to that of mary magdalene.

(three)

you are the nearness
a vein pulsing in my neck
the one who brings three
to this nightly colloquy
about my soul

51

you must have this
ubiquity thing down
for you've been around
all day and i doubt
even in this town
i'm the only one
so visited

now there's no more
daylight so you offer me
the son or the father,
ascetics wrapped in tigerhide
sun dancers, a lone castrato
even the dishonored gods
of ozymandias, whenever i decide
to refuse the world

and if i take none will you stay
by me this hour as i steer
a forklift through the vast warehouse
and begin an inventory

dust lifted on the wind

light shimmering in the lake

breath-fog both human and animal

a child's memory
seen clearly with the eye's corner
gone in the turning of the head

the only sure guide

SEEDS

this is the time of last times
when nobody speaks
of the living but only of the dead
who have not yet departed
in fact are so near in this hall
that we may as well eat the seed corn
all the seeds for next year's garden
we won't need them

we may gather in this city of refuge
to declare we believe in life
but we surely do believe in death
it's not high school any more
where one friend moves away and
everyone else comes back in the fall
now there's a restless crowd waiting
at the ferry dock down by the riverside
and so much white hair among us
a field of dandelions gone to seed

let the honored guest leave today
and everyone moves up a notch
takes another pace along the plank
high above the mortal abyss
his younger brother is now patriarch
his son a recent grandfather
his wife consoled but extraneous
in india they would have burned
her and she would have gone, willingly
perhaps, to the fire, not desiring
another round of summer flowers

the altar is almost buried in bouquets.
here and there a fallen petal expects
the next one.   i've heard some tribes
bury food with the dead so they
will have strength to travel and will not
return in the blanket of the land of death
to take back there with them everyone
they touch, even once and even
with affection, carriers of the great disease
no one heals from

the rain beats down the flowers outside
every last one will come to this
but as far back as writing goes
so very few have said anything
as big and plain as the thing itself
so it's with the lowest of expectations
we end murmured talks and filter in
to pick a spot and see if anyone can stand
behind dying blooms on a stormy day
and speak convincingly of eternity

the preacher tries, i give him that, tries hard
not just to speak joy but make it rise and move
through the hall, touching one, passing over
another for no reason, barely mentioning
one who was sown and sprouted
stood up and stepped beyond the tomb
as easily as we return to cars in the lot
a break in the weather and our midday life—
leaning on her car's roof his daughter
slowly shakes her head from side to side

WHITE HAIR

a suddenness of all colors
of none
like snowberry

or the full moon
drifting
out from behind a cloud

white hair is a solitude

high rock ice walls
shearing
white egrets standing wax candles

bright burning remnant of years
vanguard
of high-beam frost on tumbleweed

a solitude driving through the night
to get there
and move among many with whitest hair

fluffy seed balls scattered by chance
greeting each other with
eye contact and handclasp

to see a friend
walk away forever across a field
of untracked snow

DEBRIS

this space between
high and low tide
regulated by the law of salvage
and governed
by beachcombing

is that rare thing in our country
an unowned piece of land, home
of the goddess of beaches
a minor figure in the pantheon

.................wait................listen................

shake the bowl
it slops over
and rushes back

this is a test
this is only a test
if it had not been a test
your town would be destroyed
your neighbors bobbing
like corks in the flood
this is a test

entangled currents awaken her

she nears land
in a kimono of kelp ribbons
wet feathers, long black hairs
slippery to the touch
and lies down as if dropped there

the rounded bulge
could be a blue glass float
the bare skull of a drowned child
a thing that drifts away

to join a salt-rusted motorcycle
washed up on haida land
a smashed dock for oregon
thousands of screaming ghosts attached
to acres and tons of floating trash

nothing minor here—take
what you've got coming
distributed by the lady of beaches

remember her
when she is still

(an ekphrastic companion to Regina Browne's quilt "Tsunami: Flotsam" exhibited at Northwinds Arts, Port Townsend 2012)

FORECAST: COASTAL AREAS

rain, standing
in an all-night greyhound depot
waits with his suitcases—water

drips out from hinges and
puddles around his shoes

a sharpened breeze skitters his slicker

he'll ride two days and unpack all over
the bay area—i call to tell you he's coming

but you're chasing the luscious
summery girl shedding bits
of clothing as you follow

until you lose her and fat
drops spattering on the skylight
wake you in midnight

ALASKAN LYRIC

the lead gray doors of winter slide shut
with the sound of snow slumping off
the roof we hide under, as near the stove
as possible, studying travel brochures

in this town keeping up with the joneses
means having in the car at all times
clothes for three weeks, food for a week
a road atlas and a battery-driven laptop

my neighbor tells me his christmas plans
i'm gonna tie a snow shovel to the
hood of my car and drive south till nobody
knows what the hell it is.   there they call us

snowbirds.   last month i saw a duck that fell
asleep bobbing on the cold pond and woke
with its flat orange feet clutched in ice.   the next day
feathers and tracks of fox and mice.

i know it gets warm again, every year, and people
can adjust to almost anything, like roaches do.
lafcadio hearn asked the japanese how they wintered
in paper-walled houses.   *we get married.*

but what if I came here to explore my solitude?
in front of town hall there's a statue of sam mcgee
brightly lit in the darkest days—in that light
the frost glitters like moss made of diamonds

MOULTING

cicadas leave their empty shells perched on branches.
lizards, frogs, scruffy chickens.   snakes, tails
wrapped around saplings, pull the new body out
of the old.   dog fur drifts in a spring breeze.   hermit crabs
stay buried for months eating the old skeleton.

the buildings of victorian brick back up to the harbor—driftlogs
fill the spaces between, driftlogs and a young male
elephant seal.   his life is a will surrounded by won'ts.   he won't
eat or drink for a month.   he won't swim long for fear
of freezing.   he won't attract a female while his silky fur
lies around him rooted in chunks of shed skin.

he won't sleep deeply.   the motion light on the coffeeshop
will see to that.   he will meet us, one by one, as we approach
the yellow tape the police have strung around his cove.

I look into his round black eyes, into his utter lack of
nervousness about us, his ambassadorial certainty. if he crawls
further inland, the police will shut downtown's main street.   he

stretches his neck up and back, returns to my eyes. i can hear
his breath.   stiff hairs around his mouth pulsate.
i don't believe in death

ORCA

orca also known as
killer whale,
slaughterer, eats
two hundred pound seals
like popcorn, hunting them
in the kelpy canyons below the waves

ripping the thick pelt
over the rich fatty meat
again and again until blood
blooms on sea's surface
smooth above this brutal ballet

for the seals one way out: form
a writhing ball like bees around a queen
sacrificing those pushed to the outside

or scatter, race away
and hope nothing follows

and there is a third: whale satiation,
warbling notes of contentment
through jaws with four-inch teeth
letting the seals go, through today
no one will witness this cetacean charity

as we all gather on land
around a loaded to groaning buffet
thanksgiving day

OCTOPUS NURSERY

if badminton were played underwater
evolution could fill the niche of shuttlecock
with one of these

in a lovely shade of red
with pocked legs like medusa's hair
or coiled like fiddlehead ferns

if submarine christmas trees needed decoration
they could use this floating flock of rubbery tinsel
sliding along the branches
and some backlit infant jellyfish as well

and if god only wanted more octopi
but humans wanted to have a hand in that
as in everything else
then parents would bring children
to this seawatery birthing chamber
to see these babies, translucent pink tomato seeds

moving in generated currents beside mom
whose magenta head resembles a giant testicle
able to breathe and feed itself
and move with its own imperceptible power

while attaching to its perfect weirdness
as a fashion model clings to her fading beauty
by simply existing, hinting insistently
at the world's unbending magnificence

GLAMOUR

at the food bank
we wait in chairs
along either wall

forming a runway
she promenades
dazzling us

she is used to it
so used to it
by now, people

who stare at her
while pretending
not to look

how her height
commands attention
as she passes by

then the word
she hears even
when whispered

mongoloid
she pauses
at the magazines

the woman with her
asks *which one
do you want dear*

she reaches out
for vogue, for glamour
and leaves us

quieted by
the regal beauty she
always possesses

THE SACRED TEXT

in a cloistered world young monks pace
their hands nearly touching
before their hearts

but not fully joined—that
would make the texting
difficult to read

the monks look much like us
but their absorbed attention
their devotion sets them apart

when they pass one another
on the pavement stones
they do not notice or speak

they may waggle their thumbs
in rapid arcane patterns
but this is neither greeting nor recognition

they keep their eyes lowered
as if under watch by superiors
or stop still to receive the blessing

someday they will rejoin the world
but laymen wonder if the keening
of silence, after so much of it

will be all they can bear to hear

VARIATIONS ON A LULLABY

you're over 70
don't count your victories
or the hours till dawn
just sleep
let your jaw hang open
till the grandkids dare
each other to pitch pennies in
snore yourself awake
and drift back
down
to the muddy bottom
of the crawdad pond
where you played

air brakes hissing, the bus
glides into another town
my eyes spin open
i see my own face
staring back at me
while beyond the glass
an entire family huddles
on the depot bench
can't say where i am
or where i'm going
just not there yet

she's learned to park where
the angle softens
the streetlamp's glare
through windows fogged
by the boys' breathing
in the back
whoever invented bucket seats
never slept in one
footsteps pass by
she checks the locks
figures tomorrow
tries to rest

ALL OUR SORROWS

it was just dawn in a city called phoenix
the jeeplike vehicles park
a block away from the temple

the conscripts click the safeties off
directed by men in dark glasses
they approach the nest of infidels

no need to kick in an unlocked door
but they do and spray the meditation hall
with bullets—torn bodies spin to the floor

sprawl in a final prostration, defaced, stains
splatter the walls, sorrows are erased
all but one

the girl sits so still as to be wondrously
unnoticed—how could it be
that if she moved the scything slaughter

would take her too but into her calmness
no shot came?   she breathes and hears
the stutter of slugs as faraway birds, as frogs at dusk

the light of day creeps across her shoulders
her eyelids remain closed and her body
rests quietly in this world of endless sorrow

KUWAITI TOURIST BUREAU

while you were in afghanistan
hell mellowed
though the sulphur stench still lingers
in any outdoor air

the bodies (too many for jackals) have been taken
by quickly trained filipino crews
and a dark night is almost dark
a few glows on the horizon
not the torchlight flares
that once were everywhere

with our scant rain there remain
crusty dark red stains on the sand
which we hope are engine oil

much of this time has been hope
brownish waves slap the beach as before
and no more dead appear overnight--
the blue sky, the stars look down
on children whose bare thighs bear
the uranium sores called *wounds of peace*

some say peace will not last
except as prelude to greater horrors.
i say little--a quiet afternoon,
moonrise, a healthy infant,
a short memory and who knows, perhaps it will

for now, thank you for visiting
and helping us to recover
from your last visit

Finalities

SONG FOR X

i liked him best of all when his eyes
were fixed straight ahead
not looking round the room
in search of my error

he always pulled more than his share
of sheets so of course i liked
him lying still in dark red and cottony white

i liked his strength even when it left
my nose bent and my right
shoulder always a bit stiff

i liked watching him awaken
especially when he realized
everything was changed now

i liked him beginning to beg
and how smoothly the trigger slid back

best of all i liked it being over

TENDING GRAVES

he died wanting a drink
i placed on his stone a double shotglass
the rain fills and the sun evaporates

while she wanted nothing the family could give her
died wanting her high-school sweetheart
she'd turned down for the sensible secure selection
so i left a pair of crimson spike heels above her

her grandmother watched three of her four children die
in 1918 of the flu and never wanted a thing after
but for them to come back and her to feed them
with the bowl of porridge and the tiny spoon i left

and for that woman's father, who died
rather suddenly after the spanish shell exploded
trying to hold his intestines in with
both hands, wanting only to succeed in that task
and walk away whole, for him i left a blood-red sash
and the names of his two babies written on a cigar band

i don't stay here yet but sometimes
you'll see me sitting on the soft grass
or leaning against a tree asking the family spirits
to tell me what they could not release
before it was time to come here

but i can make your tending of my
grave easier: if what lingers is what i wanted
most as i died, you'll have to set
the entire story-filled earth
and every scintilla of its inhuman beauty
atop whatever uncarved stone marks my rest
and then go and be with the one you love
while the grateful dead rise and dance

JUST A HOUSE

the noise of mechanized humanity
flattens the music of poetry
but at dawn on a desert morning in june
i hear no earthmovers or sirens or
helicopters just the racket of hundreds
of quail and doves shouting about sunlight
and the birdbrained thought of getting laid
wide-eyed, flapping, fighting for balance

i used to wake and find you
near, warm, drowsy and today
i still wake, clutch the covers and watch
a writhing sundisc push above the ridge

        ***

of all the theories about stonehenge
the one everybody rejects is that
it was accidental, yet here

in this 70's tract house for a week
around the summer solstice the sun
enters the westernmost window

darts down the hallway at lightspeed
to illuminate in an alcove at hall's end
a carving of the goddess of compassion

whom almost all archaeologists
consider us to have worshipped
despite our recent behavior

        ***

in winter dusk
i open both doors
and offer the fire
chunks of desert trees

if i surrender enough
it gives back
warmth and a wiggling
dance of destruction
to watch late into the night

***

beside the western window
the palo verde tree close enough to touch
is where i spent more waking hours
than anywhere else

i settled accounts
calmed my heart and mind
with repetitive tasks
spools of different-colored threads
watched time pass
the sunset go from almost too far to see
to almost too hot to bear
the beautiful things i made turning months into years
slowly and so carefully straight to the end

***

not a florida room, not an arizona room, a screen porch
with a northern exposure where the family sat
close enough to the kitchen to talk about food
far enough away to smoke for those who did

a pool of conversation becomes
a gathering of ghosts, uncle tony with
cigar and tequila and grass and wine, did i ever
see him sober? and the grandchildren
looked younger then. your eyes catch mine, you barely
nod, there's something you want me to do. oh, yes,
live in the present.

***

it was a mexican village, you could tell by the costumes
and the church steeple, stucco and red tile. it was sunday,
you could tell by the finery and the idleness. it was always
sunday for them.

we were the only people in the village with a framed painting
hanging on the back wall of our carport. it was the first thing i saw
when i pulled into the driveway, and the last when i backed out

THE LAST BUTTERNUT SQUASH

the house burned down she said
you can't go back there
you have the things you took when you moved
but the house is gone

not quite, this evening when i reach
into the leaf-shaped centerpiece bowl
to take out the last butternut squash
grown in the garden under my bedroom window

the shell-like skin preserving
the flame-colored fleshy wall surrounding
the fibrous pulp brought sixteen hundred miles
out of which peek a few seeds

TIMBERLINE

for bryn

each word is a cairn
so you may find a way across
a surface so hard
it shows no previous track

winter snow floats down and
covers them where they stand
till spring warmth pushes them
into clear sight again

for a long time i just walked
in this far-seeing land
not caring if you knew
where you were or were going

i found my own way
you would find yours

now the journey is nearly over
suddenly i am concerned for you
with only poems to tell you everything i know

they have to be clear beyond
all interpretation and that
takes more than one try, or ten
i am sorry i did not build cairns
sooner or sit on a flat rock beside
the trail and wait for you

you'll see
it was just too beautiful
not to keep going

ANY DAY CAN END IN AN AMBULANCE RIDE

a lone maple in the meadow
disrobes before a chill wind
leaves cartwheeling across dry grass
throughout the country
old people are falling—

i have a friend who snapped
a finger against the wall
she caught herself with
to remain upright, another
who shattered a leg on the floor

of his own house, one who bending
to pet a small dog
split her forehead open
on a curbstone—falling leaves
that when green fed the growing

tree of life but red and brown and gray
are pulled away by a breezy day
given flight by gravity
and cluster in rustling clumps
while the man with a cane

remembers a child running, running

THE BACKSLIDER CONSIDERS THEOLOGY

at the moment of climax
what does an agnostic shout?
i don't know

and my unitarian sweetie
who i expected to shriek *universe*
falls back on *oh god oh jesus*

then i think of coupling satanists
surely they don't call on god
but rather beelzebub and belial

leading me to wonder
since i've never heard that
even late on a full moon

do devil-worshipers come
or is that something a merciful god
reserves for the righteous alone?

THE BACKSLIDER DEVELOPS HIS ART

OK i bought a notebook

i might have been the last writer in town
without one but now?   if i can see
by your outfit that you are a cowboy
you can see by my notebook
that i am a genuine poet

i just got tired of losing whole lyrics
or even a good phrase before i got home
so now i'm lying in wait, watching
the vast open plains of language and emotion
for the slightest movement of poetry

so far, nothing

still waiting

i'm not worried—i didn't go to the drugstore
for the 99-cent pocket-sized spiral notebook
because it's really designed for
shopping lists and phone numbers

i spent three times as much at anna's
specialized writer's store where notebooks
are uniquely enhanced with creativity
and virtually revise themselves

i swear if this doesn't work
i'll get a master's in fine arts

THE BACKSLIDER VISITS MOTHER NATURE

noontime and the town deer
laze in my neighbor's yard
under apple trees.   the young man
delivering alder and fir for heat
has a daughter and two tours in iraq
and knows to the minute when
hunting season starts tomorrow.
i wish they'd put just one foot
outside town limits in the morning.
they know too.   looking right at me
one lets a wad of undigested flowers
rise in her elevator throat. *fuck you*
she means *the pioneers called us*
steak and haunch.   now you
feed us.

***

the slugs leave a broken strand of pearls
as track upon the sidewalk, curled
and crossed as they head to hide
under the carpeting leaves of chard.
because i sleep late i ask a slug
to describe the dawn: *i don't know*
it all happened so fast

THE BACKSLIDER READS THE DIVINE COMEDY

i always expected hell
to have a huge oversupply
of politicians

not because they all deserve eternal agony
but to find there an audience so
easily persuaded

of lawyers too, who hope to uncover
the elusive two wrongs
that do make a right

but dante really fills the bleachers
with traitors, jihadis, falsifiers, advertisers,
living popsicles and men who literally talk shit

till two of heaven's glories may be room
to move without bumping some damned soul
and solitude for artistic contemplation

though all the critics agree
the crowd bound for perdition
writes livelier poetry

SAILING ACROSS SILENCE

sailing
across silence
but for the thump
of the chop
on the planks

looking back
at the wake path
once thin as the width
of the hull slithering
through the sea

now spread so
wide anyone
can follow, a poem
read over
and over

the canvas pops
in the wind
the wind knows
where it goes
not the pilot

NAME OMITTED FOR REASONS OF PRIVACY

here we have
what we've dreamed
all our lives
might be true

solar arrays on every roof
(no matter the sun
rarely shines)
each yard edible

deer dozing
in intersections
the electric cars
too quiet to wake them

live theater, our own
radio station, free
classes in everything,
weekly parades

people die and are buried
in the earth wrapped only
in a shroud, this
really happens

unitarian retirees
think they've already died
and gone to the place
where everyone is loved

though you might go for weeks
and not see a black face, years
till he tells you they're
no longer called negroes

but if you never could sing
you can warble here
if you never could act
now you know the secret
pretend

boatbuilders trade oarlocks
for shiatsu treatments, farmers
bring lavender to town and leave
with software, not a dime
changes hands

the bank is a galvanized bucket
of loose change and bills
at the end of water street
where they're building the bridge

which may well go nowhere
but at least the crew
working on this end
puts in a full day

PORTRAIT OF THE ARTIST

my sister was an only child.
my parents had distance enough between them
for two entirely other people.
i was chosen last so often at recess
the captains would argue over who had to take me.
i never had a pet that didn't soon become roadkill
if i didn't find it someone would show me where
the soft fur was pasted to the roadway
and held by the congealed blood.

as i grew so did questions in my mind:
was this the blood the priest talked about on sunday?
couldn't i just fake my biography?
would it be any worse to be a liar caught out
than it was to be me and my family?

then i discovered art--many boys found the naked maja
or greek wrestlers but for me it was a chance
to sit and write pure inventions and feel them
become as real as a severed thumb.
afterwards i can look and might not even know
who wrote this. it tells me:
go through life as if art is another body
inside which i live, where the world
seems to be more than it seems to be.

ENLIGHTENMENT FOR DUMMIES

1) o monks
be in the moment

but teacher
which moment?   this one?
or the one just past?

do not evaluate—
strive to be
in the very next moment
exactly when it arrives

"next"?
you mean there's
a next moment too?

2) don't be the doer
be the one undone

what else
do you need
to know?

3)   o monks
when people ask
are you meditating
tell them no
i'm just sitting here and
let it be true

4)   teacher
what about
death?

as you become decrepit
and lose your faculties
one by one

as it takes all day
to button your shirt in the morning
and unbutton it for bed

acomplishment
is still accomplishment

5)   christians worship this
christ but do not
follow him in stillness

buddhists do the same
with the buddha

and judaism?
who is this
judy?

6)   on my good days
i don't have an answer
for anything

7)   who am i
who do i think i am
who i am not
is that who
just is

who is this thought
that was
who is
and will be
that i just am

watch the clock
tick a tock
who am
that i
will be

SUBMISSION GUIDELINES

no cat poems, well, maybe if they're really good ones
no poems involving the burial of a dog or dogs
you may assume we don't care what you see out your window
no sexual braggadocio, even if you're female
writing about lacking the words is the worst kind of oxymoron
the aesthetic tension between light and darkness has been done
make that "has often been done", no, "has been done too often"
no last-minute changes to your manuscript
if we want, we can toss your work and not tell you, so be likeable
we owe you the courtesy of a prompt reply
in fact, have owed you that for over a year now
no gobbledygook, unless it resembles what we usually print
only one race or gender per poet
study and emulate our back issues—we don't like surprises
payment is one copy—just pass it around
OK, two, but that's it
further guidelines on our website, which is currently down

THE HERMIT'S APPEAL

because i do not travel
because it has become
more difficult to not be here

because i once drove and do not
because i walked thirty
miles in a day and now three

because everything takes more time
and there is less because i age
because i will forget, if blessed

with more years, how to run
how to stand, how to turn over
even what your name is

i have to find a nearby joy
a walk on the beach, heading home
talking of such ordinary things as

asking those i love to come now
not later, not for the memorial service
but to cross the distance i cannot

so we may meet again—i cannot
put it plainer than this—and here i
remove my poet's hat and yours as reader

to ask if these words were clipped from a page
and slid into a real envelope to whom
would you address them?

About the author

Born in Providence on Good Friday 1946, raised in Texas, I was for about a decade a poet with numerous magazine publications, and even anthologized, until in my mid-twenties poetry left me silent for about forty years. In that time I lived some years in Japan, logged on Vancouver Island and for twenty-five years ran a stone and jewelry business centered in Tucson. Several years ago writing returned and I moved north to discover what use it was to me or anyone else.

CPSIA information can be obtained
at www.ICGtesting.com
Printed in the USA
FSOW03n1852280915
11527FS